I NEED ALL THE FRIENDS I CAN GET

BY CHARLES M. SCHULZ

When the first edition of I NEED ALL THE FRIENDS
I CAN GET, written and illustrated by world-famous car-
toonist Charles M. Schulz, appeared in 1964, it enjoyed
the rare privilege of top placement on both adult and
children's best-seller lists. It followed the lead of the
1962 Schulz best seller, HAPPINESS IS A WARM PUPPY.

Now, Schulz is back with this new and enlarged
version of I NEED ALL THE FRIENDS I CAN GET, but
you'll find three times as many pages of cartoons and
sentiments.

Charlie Brown, who would "even settle for a 'fair-
weather' friend," *Snoopy,* who has all the friends he
could possibly need, and the rest of the PEANUTS®
gang are assembled again — to enlighten you with
their thoughts on the meaning of friendship.

Don't forget to ask for the new, enlarged versions of
HAPPINESS IS A WARM PUPPY, LOVE IS WALKING
HAND-IN-HAND and CHRISTMAS IS TOGETHER-
TIME, too.

A friend is someone who laughs at all your jokes.

A friend is someone who'll do your homework while you watch TV.

A friend is someone who'll speak up for you.

A friend is someone who understands sharing.

A friend is someone who answers your letters.

A friend is someone who makes you feel comfortable and relaxed.

A friend is someone who attracts the teacher's attention when you don't want her to call on you.

A friend is someone who says your winning goal wasn't "just a lucky shot."

A friend is someone you can depend on even when it's not "fair weather."

A friend is someone who remembers you on Valentine's Day.

A friend is
someone who
thinks about
marshmallow sundaes
at midnight...
just like you do.

A friend is someone who makes you laugh when you're hurting.

A friend is someone who thinks you're a good dancer.

A friend is someone who doesn't get you involved unless you want to be.

A friend is someone who eats lunch with you on your first day at a new school.

A friend is someone who leaves you alone while you're watching the "soaps."

A friend is someone who asks to see your vacation pictures.

A friend is someone who'll do anything to cheer you up.

A friend is someone who likes you as much as he likes his piano.

A friend is someone who'll massage your back.

A friend is someone who doesn't mind if you cry.

A friend is someone you can call on in an emergency.

A friend is
someone who
doesn't bug you
about every
little mistake.

A friend is someone who doesn't try to shoot you down.

A friend is someone who has respect for your possessions.

A friend is someone who doesn't invite you to his piano recital.

A friend is someone who likes the same TV programs you do.

A friend is someone who'll take care of you when you have the vapors.

A friend is someone who adds meaning to your life.

A friend is someone who doesn't gossip about you.

A friend is someone who sticks with your team...rain or shine.

A friend is someone who remembers to bring the can of balls.

A friend is someone who'll give you a free ride.

A friend is someone who tells you not to worry if you double-fault and lose the winning point.

A friend is someone who appreciates your kind of music.

A friend is someone you can telephone after midnight.

A friend is someone who'll go jogging with you at six in the morning.

A friend is someone who'll let you sulk if you feel like it.

A friend is someone who'll try to find you when you're lost.

A friend is
someone who
respects you
even though
you're not
as big.

A friend is
someone who
doesn't talk
about your
braces.

A friend is someone you can kiss on the nose.

A friend is someone who doesn't move in on your territory.

A friend is someone who doesn't laugh at you.

A friend is someone who knows when to keep quiet.

A friend is someone who doesn't tell you anything "for your own good."

A friend is someone you can trust.

A friend is someone who gets a lower grade than yours and keeps you from being the dumbest in the class.

A friend is someone who doesn't play rough.

A friend is someone who rescues you when you get yourself into a stupid situation.

CHOP
CHOP
CHOP
CHOP
CHOP

A friend is someone who gives you the hard cover edition instead of waiting for the paperback to come out.

A friend is
someone who
doesn't make fun of you
even when you do
dumb things.

A friend is someone who'll pick you up when you're down.

A friend is someone who isn't put off by your crabby face.

A friend is someone as sweet and pretty as your sister.

A friend is someone who helps you forget your self-doubts.

A friend is someone who offers to bring the dessert to your dinner party.

A friend is someone who puts you up for membership in his club.

A friend is someone who says "My treat."

A friend is someone who doesn't criticize your personal philosophy even if it's wishy-washy.

A friend is
someone who
doesn't intrude
on your solitude.

A friend is someone you can count on.